D1224312

LOOKING AT COUNTRIES

Looking at
IRAN

Kathleen Pohl

Reading consultant: Susan Nations, M.Ed.,
author/literacy coach/consultant in literacy development

Gareth Stevens
Publishing

Please visit our Web site at www.garethstevens.com.
For a free color catalog describing Gareth Stevens Publishing's list of
high-quality books, call 1-800-542-2595 (USA) or 1-800-387-3178 (Canada).
Gareth Stevens Publishing's fax: 1-877-542-2596

Library of Congress Cataloging-in-Publication Data

Pohl, Kathleen.
    Looking at Iran / Kathleen Pohl.
        p. cm. — (Looking at countries)
    Includes bibliographical references and index.
    ISBN-10: 0-8368-8768-9   ISBN-13: 978-0-8368-8768-6 (lib. bdg.)
    ISBN-10: 0-8368-8775-1   ISBN-13: 978-0-8368-8775-4 (softcover)
    1. Iran—Description and travel—Juvenile literature. I. Title.
DS254.75.P64   2008
955—dc22   2007027944

This edition first published in 2008 by
Gareth Stevens Publishing
A Weekly Reader® Company
1 Reader's Digest Road
Pleasantville, NY 10570-7000 USA

Senior Managing Editor: Lisa M. Guidone
Senior Editor: Barbara Bakowski
Creative Director: Lisa Donovan
Designer: Tammy West
Photo Researcher: Sylvia Ohlrich

Photo credits: (t=top, b=bottom, l=left, r=right)
Cover Franco Origlia/Getty Images; title page SuperStock; p. 4 Hermann Dornhege/
VISUM/The Image Works; p. 6. Vodjani/Ullstein/Peter Arnold; p. 7t Rob Howard/
Corbis; p. 7b Tor Eigeland/Alamy; p. 8 EmmePi Images/Alamy; p. 9t Morteza
Nikoubazl/Reuters/Landov; p. 9b M. Phillip Kahl/Photo Researchers; p. 10 Stefan
Noebel-Heise/Transit/Peter Arnold; p. 11t Silke Reents/VISUM/The Image Works;
p. 11b Mohammad Kheirkhah/UPI/Landov; p. 12l Raheb Homavandi/Reuters/Landov;
p. 12r Majid/Getty Images; p. 13 Earl Kowall/Corbis; p. 14 Caren Firouz/Reuters/Landov;
p. 15t Franco Pizzochero/Marka/Age Fotostock; p. 15b Michelle Falzone/Age Fotostock;
p. 16 Bernd Weissbrod/DPA/Landov; p. 17t Enric Marti/AP Images; p. 17b Vodjani/Ullstein/
Peter Arnold; p. 18 Patrick Snyder/Lonely Planet Images; p. 19t Sergio Pitamitz/Marka/
age fotostock; p. 19b SuperStock; p. 20t Gulfimages/Getty Images; p. 20b JTB Photo
Communications/Alamy; p. 21t TH Foto/StockFood; p. 21b Morteza Nikoubazl/Reuters/
Landov; p. 22 Dana Wilson/Peter Arnold; p. 23t Carl Purcell/Corbis; p. 23b SuperStock;
p. 24 Serge Sibert/Cosmos/Aurora Photos; p. 25t Xinhua/Landov; p. 25b Shehzad Noorani/
Majority World/The Image Works; p. 26 SuperStock; p. 27 SDBReligion/Alamy (2)

Printed in the United States of America

1 2 3 4 5 6 7 8 9 10 09 08 07

Contents

Words that appear in the glossary are printed in **boldface** type the first time they occur in the text.

Where Is Iran?

Iran is in southwestern Asia, in an area known as the Middle East. Iran borders seven other countries. On the west are Iraq and Turkey. Pakistan and Afghanistan border Iran on the east. To the north are Armenia, Azerbaijan (a-zer-bye-JAHN), and Turkmenistan. Iran has coasts on the Caspian Sea, the Persian Gulf, and the Gulf of Oman.

Did you know?

Iran is one of the oldest countries in the world. It was once called **Persia**. People have lived there for almost five thousand years.

Atlantic Ocean

ASIA

EUROPE

IRAN

AFRICA

Indian Ocean

Iran is part of an area known as the Middle East.

The Azadi Tower is a symbol of Iran. Some people call it the Freedom Tower. It stands in Azadi Square in the capital city, Tehran.

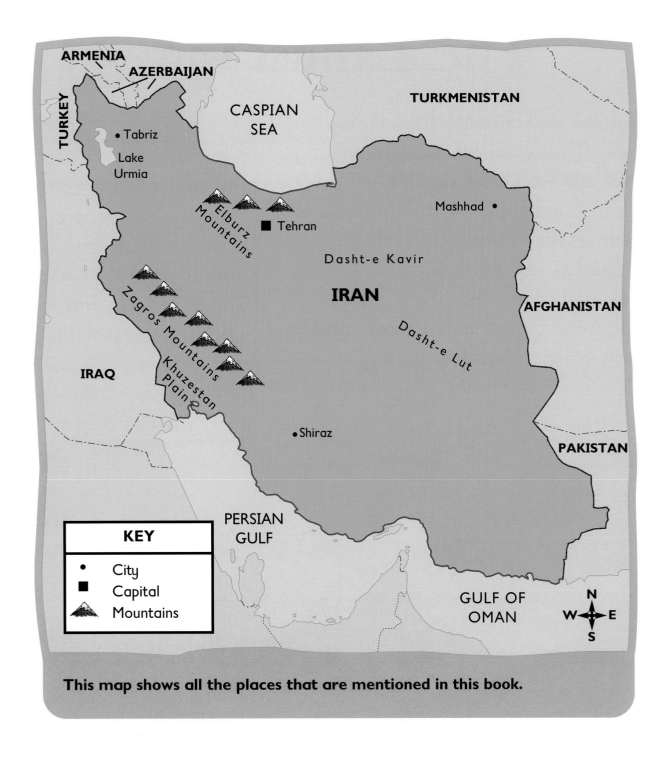

This map shows all the places that are mentioned in this book.

Tehran (tay-RAN) is the capital of Iran. It is also the country's largest city. Tehran has new buildings with tall towers. It also has very old buildings and places of prayer, called **mosques** (mahsks). Offices, schools, banks, and parks line the streets of Tehran.

The Landscape

Mountains and deserts make up most of Iran. The two main mountain ranges are the Elburz and the Zagros. Earthquakes in the mountains sometimes make the ground shake. Earthquakes can destroy cities, damage homes, and cause loss of life. Major earthquakes are rare, but small quakes happen in Iran almost every day!

Did you know?

An **oasis** is a green area in the desert where grass and other plants grow. The plants get water from underground springs.

The snowcapped Elburz Mountains are in the northern part of Iran.

Strong winds blow the hot sands of the Dasht-e Lut desert.

A high, dry **plateau**, or flat area of land, makes up the center of Iran. Few people live in this huge desert area. The Dasht-e Kavir (dahsht-ee-kuh-VEER), or Great Salt Desert, has a salty crust. Sand dunes make up the Dasht-e Lut (dahsht-ee-LOOT) desert.

Most people live in the lowlands in the north near the sea. The land and climate there are good for farming.

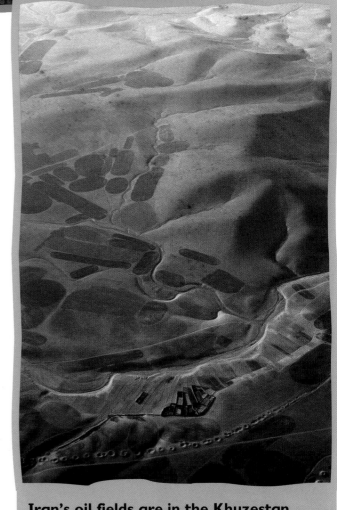

Iran's oil fields are in the Khuzestan Plain, along the Persian Gulf.

Weather and Seasons

Most of Iran is very dry. It has few lakes and streams with freshwater for drinking. Most of them dry up in the hot summer. The greatest rainfall is in the north near the Caspian Sea. Very little rain falls in most other parts of the country. The rainiest season is winter, from November through March.

Did you know?

Since ancient times, people in Iran have used a water supply system called a **qanat** (or kanat). It collects underground water and moves it through tunnels to places where people need it.

Iran gets little rainfall. Qanats help people by moving water to places that need it.

People enjoy skiing in the Elburz Mountains in winter.

Lake Urmia is a salt lake. It is one of the few lakes in Iran that does not dry up in the heat.

Summers are coolest in the mountains. In the south, along the Persian Gulf, summers are hot and damp. Strong winds blow hot, dry air from the west across central Iran in summer.

Winters in the mountains can be very cold and can bring plenty of snow and ice. Spring and fall are mostly mild.

Iranian People

About sixty-five million people live in Iran. Almost all of them are **Muslims**, people who follow the religion of **Islam**. The government of Iran is based on the rules of Islam.

The law of Islam tells people how to dress and behave. Men and women must sit apart on a bus or a subway. They stand in separate lines in stores. Beaches and ski slopes have different areas for men and women. Many women wear a long veil, called a **chador**, when they are in public.

In public, girls and women must cover their hair and wear clothes that cover the body. Only the face, toes, and hands are allowed to be seen.

Women can sit in female-only cars of subway trains.

A crowd of Muslims gathers in front of a mosque to pray.

All Muslims must pray at five different times each day. Friday is the Islamic holy day of the week. Offices and schools are closed.

School and Family

Children must go to primary school for five years, beginning at age six. Boys and girls go to separate schools. They study math, science, and Islam. They learn **Persian**, the language of Iran. The school year runs from September through June. At the end of primary school, all students take a test. Those who pass the test can attend a three-year middle school.

Some students then go to a four-year trade school or an academic high school. Students who want to go to college must take a national exam. Iran has more than thirty free public colleges that train students for jobs in medicine, teaching, and other careers.

Students study the Koran, the holy book of Islam.

In Iran, children go to primary school for five years.

Many Iranian families are large. Children, parents, and grandparents gather for meals. The food is served on a cloth spread over a carpet.

Did you know?

The most studied book in school is the **Koran**. It is the holy book of Islam.

Most families are large. Grandparents often live with their children and grandchildren. The father is the head of the household. The mother usually cooks, cleans, and cares for the children. In the country, women help with farm chores, too. In the cities, some women have jobs outside the home.

Country Life

One of every three people in Iran lives in the country. Most of them are farmers. Some use modern tractors to farm. Others use mules. Farmers grow wheat, barley, rice, and nuts. Figs, dates, melons, olives, and spices are other farm products. Near the Caspian Sea, many people fish.

Many farmers grow fruits or nuts. This man is harvesting dates from a date palm tree.

Fishermen catch large fish in nets in the Caspian Sea. They sell the fishes' eggs, called caviar (KA-vee-ahr).

This village is one of the oldest towns in Iran. It is known for its red soil and clay buildings.

Some villages in Iran do not have power for lights. They do not have running water. People take baths in a public bath in the town square.

Some people who live in the country are **nomads**. They move from place to place to **graze** their goats and sheep.

City Life

Most people in Iran live and work in cities. About twelve million people live in Tehran. More than half of them were born somewhere else, though. Tehran's streets are crowded with cars, buses, and taxis. The city is home to Iran's main airport.

Did you know?

For thousands of years, traders traveled on the **Silk Road** through Iran. Some of Iran's big cities are on the old path.

Cars, buses, and taxis crowd the busy streets of Tehran.

16

People shop at large bazaars, like this one in Tehran. They buy food, handmade rugs, and other crafts.

Mashhad is a large city and a major trade center in the east. Tabriz (tah-BREEZ), in the northwest, is famous for its **bazaar**. That is a market where people buy and sell food and goods. Weavers make and sell fine rugs at the bazaar in Tabriz.

Many cities blend the old with the new. In the old parts of towns are mosques and marketplaces. The new areas have big shops, modern apartment buildings, and wide streets.

Many visitors come to this garden in the old city of Shiraz.

Iranian Houses

Most homes in the country are square houses made of sun-dried mud bricks. The houses have only one or two rooms. A single room may be used as a bedroom, a dining room, and a sitting room. Most houses have no windows and are topped by flat roofs. In villages, people like to sit on their flat roofs and visit. At the center of most villages is a mosque.

This man is making mud bricks. Many homes in Iran are built of the sun-dried blocks.

Did you know?

Most homes in Iran do not have tables and chairs. People sit on cushions on the floor to eat their meals.

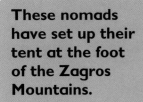
These nomads have set up their tent at the foot of the Zagros Mountains.

Many people live in modern apartment buildings in big cities, such as Tehran.

Nomads live in tents, which they take with them when they travel. The tents are made of animal skins or goat hair.

In the cities, many people live in modern apartments. Most are made of brick or cement.

Iranian Food

People in Iran eat bread with most meals. They serve rice with vegetables or cover it with a thick sauce. **Dolma** is a popular dish. It is made with vegetables or grape leaves that are stuffed with rice and meat.

Iranians eat lamb, beef, and fish. They do not eat pork, because Islam forbids it. Fruits, such as melons and dates, and nuts are favorite foods, too.

Dolmas are grape leaves stuffed with ground meat and rice.

Lamb kebabs are a popular meal in Iran. The meat is cooked with vegetables on a stick.

Did you know?

Chai is the word for "tea" in Iran.

This seller serves tea and snacks at a city bazaar.

Teenagers everywhere like to eat at fast-food restaurants!

Many people enjoy eating at restaurants. They go to teahouses to drink tea and visit with friends. A drink made with yogurt, or sour milk, is popular, too.

At Work

Some people in Iran work in banks, schools, and offices. Others are doctors and nurses in hospitals.

In the Persian Gulf area, many people work in the oil business. About one hundred wells are drilled in Iran each year. Oil is one of the main products Iran sells to other countries. Other important goods are fruits, nuts, spices, fish eggs, and rugs.

Iran is known for its silk cloth. Silk thread is made by caterpillars called silkworms. Farmers in northwestern Iran raise silkworms for their silk.

Did you know?

Iran is known all over the world for its beautiful rugs.

Huge ships carry oil out of the Persian Gulf.

Weavers dry their handmade rugs in the sun.

Workers in Shiraz, in southern Iran, make fine metal bowls and vases.

People work in **factories**, too. They make bricks, cement, cloth, and leather goods. In ports on the coasts, people load ships with goods to be sent to other countries.

Having Fun

Nowruz (now-ROOZ) is the New Year's holiday in Iran. It starts on the first day of spring and lasts for thirteen days. Shops and schools are closed. Families visit each other, eat sweets and nuts, and give gifts. On the thirteenth day, people go outdoors for a picnic. They also enjoy music and dancing.

Did you know?

Soccer is hugely popular in Iran. Fans crowd into Azadi Stadium in Tehran to watch the national team play matches.

Families observe Nowruz (the New Year's holiday) with a picnic. It is bad luck to stay inside on the last day of this thirteen-day-long celebration.

Playing and watching sports are popular activities. Favorite sports include soccer, basketball, volleyball, wrestling, and polo. People also like to hike and ski in the mountains.

Many people in Iran enjoy listening to the radio. They also watch television and go to movies. Chess is a popular game to play with friends.

A young soccer fan cheers at a match.

Children enjoy playing on a swing set in their village.

Iran: The Facts

- Iran is an Islamic **republic**. The country's official name is the Islamic Republic of Iran. It is ruled by religious leaders.

- Iran has a president, who is elected by the people.

- Iran is divided into thirty regions. Each has its own capital city and government.

- Men and women in Iran who are at least fifteen years old may vote in the country's elections.

- Persian, or Farsi, is the language of Iran.

The flag of Iran has three bars—green, white, and red. The Arabic words for "God is great" are written along the edges of the green and red bars. The national symbol is in the middle of the white bar.

The Iranian unit of money is the **rial** (ree-AHL).

People in Iran have woven beautiful rugs for 2,500 years.

Did you know?

When creating rugs, weavers often make a mistake—on purpose! They want to show their belief that "only God is perfect."

Glossary

bazaar – an outdoor marketplace where food and other goods are bought and sold

chador – a long body veil worn by women in Iran to cover themselves in public

dolma – a dish of vegetables or grape leaves stuffed with rice and meat

factories – buildings where workers make goods

graze – to put animals out to eat grass in fields

Islam – the religion of Muslims

kebabs – cubes of meat cooked with vegetables on a stick

Koran – the holy book of Islam

mosques – Islamic houses of prayer

Muslims – people who follow the teachings of Muhammad, the founder of Islam

nomads – people who don't live in one place but wander from place to place to find food or graze their animals

oasis – a green place in the desert, fed by underground springs, where plants grow

Persia – the ancient name of modern-day Iran

Persian – the modern language of Iran; also known as Farsi

plateau – a high, flat area of land

qanat – an underground system of tunnels to transport water

Ramadan – a holy month of fasting observed by Muslims, when they do not eat or drink during daylight hours

republic – a kind of government in which decisions are made by the people of the country and their representatives

rial – unit of currency, or money, in Iran

Silk Road – an ancient trade route that crossed the land that is modern-day Iran

Find Out More

Enchanted Learning
www.enchantedlearning.com/geography/mideast

Encyclopedia FunTrivia
www.funtrivia.com/en/Geography/Iran-6494.html

Fact Monster: Kids from Iran
www.factmonster.com/ipka/A0932447.html
www.factmonster.com/ipka/A0107640.html

KidsKonnect: Iran Fast Facts
www.kidskonnect.com/Iran/IranHome.html

Publisher's note to educators and parents: Our editors have carefully reviewed these Web sites to ensure that they are suitable for children. Many Web sites change frequently, however, and we cannot guarantee that a site's future contents will continue to meet our high standards of quality and educational value. Be advised that children should be closely supervised whenever they access the Internet.

My Map of Iran

Photocopy or trace the map on page 31. Then write in the names of the countries, bodies of water, cities, land areas, mountains, and deserts listed below. (Look at the map on page 5 if you need help).

After you have written in the names of all the places, find some crayons and color the map!

Countries
Afghanistan
Armenia
Azerbaijan
Iran
Iraq
Pakistan
Turkey
Turkmenistan

Bodies of Water
Caspian Sea
Gulf of Oman
Lake Urmia
Persian Gulf

Cities
Mashhad
Shiraz
Tabriz
Tehran

Land Areas, Mountains, and Deserts
Dasht-e Kavir
Dasht-e Lut
Elburz Mountains
Khuzestan Plain
Zagros Mountains

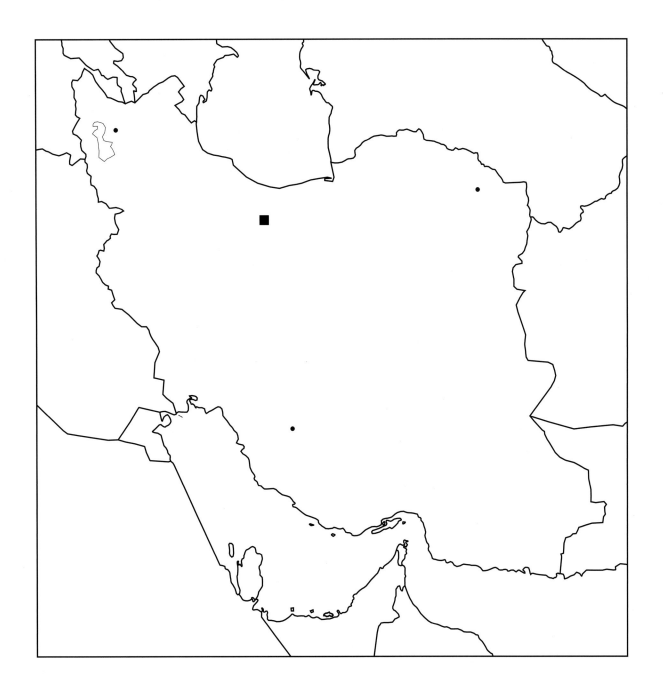

Index